Pet Questions and Answers

CATS

Questions and Answers

by Christina Mia Gardeski

raintree
a Capstone company — publishers for children

Raintree is an imprint of Capstone Global Library Limited, a company incorporated in England and Wales having its registered office at 264 Banbury Road, Oxford, OX2 7DY – Registered company number: 6695582

www.raintree.co.uk
myorders@raintree.co.uk

Edited by Carrie Braulick Sheely and Alesha Halvorson
Designed by Kayla Rossow
Picture research by Pam Mitsakos
Production by Gene Bentdahl

ISBN 978 1 4747 2143 1 (hardback)
20 19 18 17 16
10 9 8 7 6 5 4 3 2 1

ISBN 978 1 4747 2155 4 (paperback)
21 20 19 18 17
10 9 8 7 6 5 4 3 2 1

British Library Cataloguing in Publication Data
A full catalogue record for this book is available from the British Library.

Every effort has been made to contact copyright holders of material reproduced in this book. Any omissions will be rectified in subsequent printings if notice is given to the publisher.

All the internet addresses (URLs) given in this book were valid at the time of going to press. However, due to the dynamic nature of the internet, some addresses may have changed, or sites may have changed or ceased to exist since publication. While the author and publisher regret any inconvenience this may cause readers, no responsibility for any such changes can be accepted by either the author or the publisher.

Acknowledgements
Getty Images: Akimasa Harad, 21; Shutterstock: Benjamin Albiach Galan, 5, deftrender, 9, Ermolaev Alexander, 19, makar, 1, 22, maradon 333, 7, Maria Jeffs, cover, Nataliia Dvukhimenna, 13, PearlNecklace, 15, turlakova, 17; Thinkstock, sduben, 11

Printed and bound in China.

Contents

Who can see in the dark?

My cat!

Cats feel in the dark with whiskers. Their eyes see well in low light. They play at dawn and dusk.

Why do cats miaow?

Kittens miaow to tell their mother they need care. A fully grown cat miaows at its owner. It might want to eat or be stroked. Fully grown cats do not usually miaow at other cats.

How long do cats sleep for?

Cats sleep for most of the day. They can sleep for more than 15 hours each day. This helps them to save energy for play.

Why do cats hiss and purr?

Cats hiss when they are angry or scared. Cats often purr when they are happy. But they may also purr when they are sick or worried.

What do cats eat?

Cats are meat eaters. They get meat from wet or dry cat food. Cats need fresh water every day.

Does my cat need a bath?

Do you have a bath after dinner?

Cats do! They lick themselves

clean with their tongues.

You do not need to give your cat

a bath.

What are fur balls?

When a cat licks itself, some fur sticks to its tongue. The cat swallows this fur. It makes a ball of fur. The cat throws up the fur ball.

Do cats stay inside or go outside?

Some cats like to stay inside.

Most cats like to go outside.

They go out to hunt and play.

Some people even walk their cats
on a lead!

How do cats land on their feet?

Cats like to climb. When they jump down, their flexible bodies turn in the air. Their front paws go forwards and land first. Nice landing!

Glossary

dawn time of day when sunlight first begins to appear

dusk time when day turns into night and the sky begins to get darker

energy strength to do active things without getting tired

flexible able to bend

fur ball ball of fur that lodges in a cat's stomach; fur balls are made of fur swallowed by a cat as it grooms itself

lead length of material or cord attached to a collar, used for holding and walking an animal

purr low, rolling sound a cat makes

whisker one of the long hairs growing near the sides of a cat's nose, used to feel

worried uneasy about something

Read more

Care for your Kitten (RSPCA Pet Guide), RSPCA (HarperCollins, 2015)

First Book of Cats, Isabel Thomas (A&C Black Childrens & Educational, 2014)

Kitty's Guide to Caring for your Cat (Pets' Guides), Anita Ganeri (Raintree, 2015)

Websites

www.cats.org.uk/cat-care/cats-for-kids
Find out some fascinating feline facts, take part in fun activities and games and get useful cat care advice.

www.rspca.org.uk/adviceandwelfare/pets/cats
Find out more about owning a cat.

Comprehension questions

1. How can you tell if a cat is angry or scared?
2. Why do cats get fur balls?

Index